A BLESSED
SECOND CHANCE

MY JOURNEY FROM DISABLED
TO FAITH-ABLED

By
Konya Maria Crippen With
Keshawn A. Spence

© Copyright 2018 Keshawn A. Spence
ISBN 978-0-578-40798-2

All rights reserved. No part of this publication may be reproduced, stored in a retrieval system, or transmitted in any form or by any means – electronic, mechanical, photocopy, recording, or any other – except for brief quotations in printed reviews, without the prior written permission of the author.

Published by KSpence, LLC
P.O. Box 2932 Virginia Beach, VA 23450

Table of Contents

Foreword 1
Chapter 1 2
Chapter 2 6
Chapter 3 10
Chapter 4 12
Chapter 5 15
Chapter 6 20
Chapter 7 22
Chapter 8 25
Chapter 9 27
Chapter 10 37
Chapter 11 41
Chapter 12 43
Chapter 13 45
Chapter 14 49
Chapter 15 50
Chapter 16 61
Psalm 91 (KJV) 63
Psalm 119: 65-72 (KJV) 65

Foreword

Dedicated to my children, Konya, Keon and Keshawn, grandchildren, sisters and loved ones. I began this book on May 2, 2009, the story of my life up to the age of 58 and the blessings God has granted me throughout my life. Some of the events toward the latter part of my life occurred as I was writing this book.

How was I kept through all of the valleys of trials and tribulations and climbed the rough side of the mountains? It's simple. Unless your belief system can withstand pressure, pain and criticism, you have to keep the faith to endure.

Chapter 1

I was born on November 25, 1959 and was raised in Stockton, Maryland by my mother, Virginia Mary Crippen, in a single parent home. I have three sisters and one brother. Out of five children, I was the middle child; my sister Ramona and brother Clay were older than me. My sisters Coya and Carol were younger than me. My mom named me Konya after a city in Turkey. She did her best to raise us well but working and caring for us really left her no time to rest and relax. I don't recall attending church every Sunday. However, I do remember all of us on our knees reciting the Lord's Prayer and thanking God for taking us through another day every night before bed.

As children we sometimes feel as if our parents are mean or too protective of us. My mom loved us equally and didn't want us to suffer through the heartaches of life or make the wrong choices in life. Don't ever think your parents don't love you because God chastises those who He loves: "For whom the Lord loveth he chasteneth, and scourgeth every son whom he receiveth" (Hebrews 12:16 KJV). Our parents love us unconditionally, just like our heavenly father. No matter what I did, I could always depend on my mom.

The new generation of children are completely different. They show no respect for their elders and walk around shooting one another. I'm glad Mom doesn't have to deal with this new generation. My brother and sisters were enough to make a car run without a battery. Out of all of my siblings, however, I was the child who stayed in trouble and was the most mischievous. Seems like everything I was told not to do I did. As the scripture states, "For the good that I would I do not: but the evil which I would not, that I do" (Romans 7:19 KJV). Praise God I was finally maturing and getting older. As 2 Timothy 3:7 (KJV) reads, I was, "Ever learning, and never able to come to the knowledge of the truth."

At the age of 15, I conceived my first child. Mom came to my rescue again and delivered my baby. From my lips to yours, Jesus was right there with me. Twelve hours of hard labor, natural childbirth, nothing for the pain and no medical doctors; just God and Mom. Praise God, thank you Lord for my mother. She delivered my daughter Konya on September 11, 1976 at 10:48 PM. I was in labor all day and exhausted by the time the pains were five minutes apart. Mom had to raise my legs and put me in a child birth position. My mother smoked a pack and a half of cigarettes during the delivery of my daughter from 11 in the morning to almost 11 at night.

Finally, the baby arrived and Mom cut the umbilical cord and tied the naval. God had blessed her hands because everything she did was right. I immediately fell sleep and Mom took care of the baby. I didn't make it to the hospital until the next day sometime that afternoon. When I arrived at the hospital, doctors told Mom that if anything were wrong with me or the child that she could be arrested because she did not have a midwife license. I became so angry; what was Mom supposed to do? It was my first child and I didn't know how much pain I was going to endure alone.

Thank you, God, for I could not have done it without you. All nine months I had to attend a high-risk clinic because I have epilepsy. Being pregnant, I could not take medications to prevent the seizures. Doctors had discussed with me the possibility of losing me and the baby if I had a seizure during labor. Yes, even before I knew Jesus as my personal Savior, He still was loving and watching over me.

Seems like this would have been enough to turn me around from being a troubled soul but it wasn't. I was going down the road to destruction again. At the age of 16, I was smoking marijuana. My boyfriend was a dealer, and what better way to get it free? Walking completely in darkness, I felt as if I had it made. Even though Satan had gained control over my mind so easily, I never gave God nor the devil a second thought. Still my Savior Jesus Christ loved me and allowed me to continue with my life. At the age of 18, I had given birth to my second child, Francis Keon Spence. We lived in Ocean City, Maryland at the time.

At the age of 20, I lost my mother; she died from complications from tuberculosis and fluid around her heart. She never approved of my boyfriend but that didn't matter to me. I had to have my own way. The more she tried to keep us apart the closer we became. Two days after I buried my mom, I married the same man Mom warned me about. We married in a cottage in Ocean City. It was a small ceremony with just the preacher and his wife and our kids.

Before Mom's death, my brother and sisters and I lived in Ironshire with my mom. After her death, we lost the house and it was torn down. All of my siblings lived with my husband and me at one time or another. After Mom's death, we all were left here with nothing, or we felt as though we had nothing. The saying is a hard head makes a soft bottom.

Oh, precious sweet Savior, yet you still loved me. Do I deserve such kind, forgiving love? In His word, He says He'll never leave nor forsake me: "Let your conversation be without covetousness; and be content with such things as ye have: for he hath said, I will never leave thee, nor forsake thee" (Hebrews 13:5 KJV).

Spiritually, I was alone in the world and didn't want anyone to talk to me about the Lord. But I definitely know better now. Trust me, I'm just a nobody trying to tell everybody about somebody who wants to save everybody.

Chapter 2

Let's go a little further; now I'm 23 years old. A mother of three. I cannot say what really happened to me because it has not been revealed to me. All I can say is what I've been told.

In August 1982 or 1983 (I'm not sure of the year), I was taken to Peninsula General Hospital in Salisbury, Maryland. Following a severe bruise to my head, I started having seizures one after another. When the doctors were able to stop the seizures, I slipped into a coma. From what I was told, I just lied there in a silent state of mind, unaware of what was going on, not knowing anything, or anyone.

I've been told that I was flown to Johns Hopkins in Baltimore. I don't know how long I was there before being sent back to Peninsula General Hospital, where I stayed for months. Eventually, I was moved to Deer's Head, a hospice hospital located in Salisbury.

Doctors believed that I would be a vegetable for the rest of my life if I ever came out of the coma. They didn't think I would live to reach the age of 25. Throughout this ordeal people were praying for me. This reminds me of the following Bible verses: "Is any sick among you? let him call for the elders of the church; and let them pray over him, anointing him with oil in the name of the Lord: And the prayer of faith shall save the sick, and the Lord shall raise him up; and if he have committed sins, they shall be forgiven him." (James 5:14-15 KJV). God blessed me and said, "My child arise." I awoke from that deep sleep but later experienced a stroke. During this time, I remained in a vegetative state.

I couldn't do anything for myself. I was not of a sound mind and had no use of my limbs, unable to talk, walk, eat or groom myself. Still the Lord was working His miracles in my life. Only then did I think once or twice about Jesus. I was the youngest person in Deer's Head at this time. After I started therapy, still with an unstable mind, I would rebel against the people that tried to help me. I would physically fight and bite people. I was known for leaving teeth marks because I bit people so hard.

Soon after, I was able to acknowledge who certain people were, mainly my children. One day a pastor asked me what was most important to me. I answered, "My children." He said, "No child; God has to be first in your life. God has to be your first love, then your children. Keep God first and everything will work out."

My doctors would let me go home on the weekends. I would go home, and upon returning my doctor would ask me, "Konya what did you do this weekend?" I would never give her an honest answer or tell her anything I did. However, nothing done in the dark will stay hidden forever. I turned up pregnant, and still without a sound mind. Here I am a mother of three, pregnant again, unable to walk, care for myself, my other children, and unable to live an independent life. This presented another risk toward my recovery. It really hurt my doctor because I had made a miraculous recovery since the coma and stroke. I was again living on the edge. Doctors suggested to my husband that I have the baby taken before the fetus was completely formed. I had fallen down so many times while on my home visits that I'd have to stay on the ground until someone came that was physically able to lift me up off the ground. My children were 3 months old, 3 years old and 6 years old. They were not able to help me off the ground. Again, I could not even take care of the kids I already had. How was I going to take care of this one? I was determined to live and to go forward in life. With my stubbornness, love and compassion in my heart, I really wanted my child and decide to keep it, even if it was a choice of my life for the baby's. My husband thought I was thinking irrationally and my doctor was disappointed. If I had been honest with her from the beginning, she could have given me something to protect me from getting pregnant.

I ended up losing the baby but somehow the faith that I had in God helped me deal with my emotions. I experienced emotional and external wounds after I found out papers were signed to abort my child and to approve a surgical procedure to prevent me from having any more children. Again, I was filled with anger and hatred. Not toward God, but toward my husband, who gave his permission to have this procedure done. What right does another human being have to play God with my life?

During this period of my life, only God and the Holy Spirit could comfort me. I actually hated all men for what one man had done to me. Through time, prayers, and just turning it all over to the Lord, I've been able to persevere.

I know I didn't do it on my own. It came from a higher power.

I had a good idea of who God was now. I was learning and getting knowledge of him. I moved in with Miss Geraldine Morris; she was the mother of the church I attended. I participated in church services seven days a week, sometimes twice a day. This was more than I ever realized you could attend church. Finally, I decided to give it all to the Lord. At the age of 26, I surrendered my life to Christ. Another soul saved, hallelujah!

Chapter 3

By this time, I was sent to Maryland Rehabilitation Center in Baltimore, Maryland. Learning to live a life with a disability was mentally challenging for me. When I arrived at the rehabilitation center in Baltimore, for the first time, I understood that my mental challenges were small compared to those of others. It made me realize that even though I'm different I've got so much to be thankful for.

I saw people who were without their limbs, no hands or feet to use. I used to complain about shoes, but when I realized how blessed I was, material things became unimportant. During this time, I met a woman named Janice Jackson who was a paraplegic, paralyzed from her neck down. Despite being paralyzed, her faith in God always shined upon her face. She was and still is an angel of mercy. She's an inspiration to me. God brought her into my life to show me the way.

Between classes and lunch, she would always go to the hospital chapel to take time to talk with God and give praise and thank Him. Pretty soon I found myself always spending spare time in the chapel. I used it is as my escape place. I changed both physically and spiritually. When the devil loses a soul, that's really when the trials and tribulations come. However, I'd always run from my problems only to find myself in the same type of situation, just in a different place. Each time I found myself back at the cross, seeking God's help, when finally, I realized running wasn't helping. I decided to give in: "Trust in the Lord with all thine heart; and lean not unto thine own understanding" (Proverbs 3:5 KJV). "For thou hast delivered my soul from death: wilt not thou deliver my feet from falling, that I may walk before God in the light of the living?" (Psalms 56:13 KJV).

When I was in the rehabilitation center, my walk was really off- balance. I would push the clients that were in wheelchairs to help keep my balance. Everyone there had a disability. I never bothered to ask them about their disability because we all were there to get better. Throughout my stay at the rehabilitation center, the staff wanted to train me for custodial work. I refused, for I knew I could do better. I worked as a maid for several years before my sickness. Because I didn't agree with their decisions for my future, I was told that I had to leave and go back home.

When I returned back home, I didn't go back to the home that I lived in before my hospitalization. I refused to allow the devil to take a foothold in my life again. I wanted my life to be surrounded by God and all about God. I just had to move on.

Chapter 4

I returned to Pocomoke, Maryland and lived with my aunt Louvinia Phillips and her daughter Liz. Mom Lou was a foster parent and the only family I had on my father's side. She loved me and accepted me as I was. I eventually started working as a hostess at Paul Revere's Smorgasbord in Ocean City. I also volunteered at Hartley Hall nursing home in Pocomoke.

Because I was disabled, I was able to live in a senior citizen building. I attended bible studies at church every week. My knowledge and spiritual foundation were growing. God was still blessing me.

I helped many of the residents that lived in the senior citizen complex. This gave me a feeling of usefulness. I was starting to live an independent life. I attended Macedonia Baptist Church in Pocomoke and taught Sunday school for children ages eight through eleven. God was still blessing me. When you start living a Godly life, however, beware because the trials and tribulations will not be far behind.

I had met a man singing in the church choir. He had a voice like an angel and was very artistic. There was no task he could not conquer, except for me. I used to work with him painting and loading trucks at the Campbell Soup Company. Physical labor was something I had done since I was 8 years old. I preferred to earn my money working with my skills rather than just having a man give it to me. Everyone always told me, "if a man gives you something, he wants something in return."

This spiritual singing man was just that. Underneath the façade of his heavenly voice, he was a worldly person. He became infatuated with me. He stalked me. I don't know how but one time he used my TV remote and telephone and could pick up on my phone calls when he was at his home. He also drew or copied my door key and had a duplicate made. After all that I'd been through, there was no way another man was going to get the best of me. I was still angry with men in general. I eventually took him to court and the judge ordered him to stay away from me.

I moved away from Pocomoke and went back to Berlin following this incident. I used to live in Berlin back in the seventies. This time I moved into a nice apartment complex located on 211 Williams Street. In the early 90's, it seemed like they were building sections or areas mainly for low-income African Americans. I don't care what town you visited; all of the black residents lived in certain sections of the towns. Even though I'm African American, I didn't want to live in the mist of my kind. I've consistently asked myself: Why do I feel this way? My people tear each other down instead of helping each other up. When I attended Lynn Haven Baptist Church, my son and I were the only African-Americans in the congregation. They helped me and accepted me before my own did. When I moved back to Berlin, I attended First Baptist Church in Berlin. I attended this church until 1998.

A BLESSED SECOND CHANCE

These lovely people helped me in many ways. They were blessings in my life and God worked through them. The whole congregation accepted my son and I with unconditional love. Pastor Taylor and his family would invite my son into their home every other weekend. Deacons of the church even helped me with the upkeep of my home. Every summer Keon was able to attend a football camp. God clearly uses all of His children, not just the ones that share the same race.

Chapter 5

During the following year, I helped Mrs. Elva Purnell often, who everyone called by her nickname "Snub". She was the mother of one of my high school classmates. I enjoyed visiting with her every day because she was homebound and restricted to her wheelchair. Snub received dialysis treatments for her kidneys twice a week and she couldn't walk, completely unable to live an independent life. She lived with her husband Tom, who was around 92 years old. My daughter had a child by Snub's grandson, who she raised like her own son. It was almost like we were family. Because of my own personal experiences, I wanted better for my daughter than what I went through in my life. As a result, I ended up marrying William, Snub's son; he was also my daughter's boyfriend's father. I married William so that my daughter would not make a mistake in marrying William's son, a man that I believed was not good enough for her. By now she was pregnant with his second child and was not receiving any help from him. No greater love has no man than a man that will lay his life down for a friend. My daughter was not only my child but also my friend. I would do anything to save her from going through what I went through.

A BLESSED SECOND CHANCE

Leave the Future Open

Leave the future open.
In case God has a plan.
So, you can say yes to him.
Take me as you can.
To a place where you would have me to do what you would do.
Take me there and show me.
I will work therein with you.
For if we clutter up our lives with things that we would plan and do not leave a place therein to do what he'd do then ...
We'll find ourselves misguided and fully out of sync.
But if we leave some space for him our minds through his can think.
So, leave the future open.
Let God enter in.
And you will have a future bright.
For he will dwell therein.

Konya Maria Crippen

<u>Now and Forever</u>

Guide me God from day to day.
Whatever I do whatever I say.
Help lift me up wherever I fall.
Help me find some good and all.
Through the darkest nights and sunlit days.
Help me rejoice and sing your praise.
And always help me be
your loving child eternally.

A BLESSED SECOND CHANCE

To My Daughter

My darling call Konya,

Although I missed out on all the important child rearing days of your life, please know that it was not of my own doing. When you needed me most, I was fighting for my life and it was only God's will that brought me through. Now you are all grown up with children of your own, yet I still try to protect you as a mother does her child. You will always be my baby. That will never change. I know you may never understand; there's many things I still don't understand. But I've learned to accept it and allow God's will to be manifested in my life. I used to question God and say why me?

"It is good for me that I have been afflicted; that I might learn thy statutes" (Psalm 119:71 KJV). "Before I was afflicted I went astray: but now I have kept thy word" (Psalm 119:67 KJV).

Over the years, I have watched you grow and bloom. The one thing God knows is our heart. To this day I still don't know what actually happened in my life, but my love I never neglected or left you of my free will. I want you to know that. I try not to dwell on my tragedies of life. For if I did, I would die daily. Everything happens for a reason. For all that has happened to me, I count it as a joy and blessings as a gift from the Lord. Sweetie, you keep your distance from me, for whatever the reason. This may be your way of protecting yourself from me. But sweetie, I won't give up; I cannot change our past but can make my future better than yesterday. Even if I never succeed, God knows I kept on trying. I gave it my best

God knows the aching of my heart; every time I reach out to you, I get rejected. At night I pray and wet my pillow with my tears. Despite my despair, I eventually end up drifting off to sleep.

Then God allows me to arise to a new day. And I start over again. I will never give up. I ask God to give me the strength to conquer obstacles in my life.

Chapter 6

Keshawn was 3 months old when I became ill in 1982. Miss Evelyn, his grandmother and my mother-in-law, took Keon and Keshawn and cared for them. When I was well enough to live an independent life, I missed my children; they were my desire to live. I prayed to God: "Out of my three children, God please let me have at least one of them back." I didn't pick any certain child but God gave me Keon. Keon was the one I was blessed to raise. I raised him up in the church. Miss Evelyn raised Keshawn up in the church. Miss Ionia raised Konya up in the church. All of my children were raised in the presence of the Lord.

"Train up a child in the way he should go: and when he is old, he will not depart from it" (Proverbs 22:6 KJV). God has blessed me to see my son Keshawn, who was a few months old at the time, graduate from high school and later on join the Navy. As I've mentioned earlier, his grandmother raised him from his infancy. Now he is grown, and for reasons that I don't understand, we are still not that close. Even though I don't worry about it anymore, it still hurts. God knows my pain but helps me endure all of my misunderstandings. I'm an outcast; well that's how I feel. If I let my rejection from my children control me, I would be dying daily.

Keshawn, I have nothing but love for you and God's grace. Good luck. You've hurt me, but I hold no grudges. Now you're a young man and a father. I'll never forget Christmas 2008 when I met your son and he was 2 years old. I told you then you'll never hurt my feelings again. When I asked could I take your son home with me, you replied: "I don't let my son go with just anybody." Wow! Thank you. I'll know better next time.

When it comes to my children, I'm all cried out but the hurt and pain makes me stronger. It encourages me to go on. I have to stay spiritual. Everything bad that's been done to me will be returned to the sender. Do unto others, as you want them to do unto you.

Even though I attempt to love my children, rejection hurts. However, I rather have honesty than to pretend. Speak openly; tell me your true feelings. I can take it. I'm stronger than you give me credit for. If God be for me, He is more than the world against me. Thank you, Jesus.

Chapter 7

In 1993, I left Berlin and moved to Newark, Delaware and would soon marry William, my grandchildren's grandfather. William and I graduated from the same high school. After a year of his traveling back and forth, sometimes I'd travel to Wilmington, where he lived with his cousin. For some reason I was letting my emotions control me. After dating for over a year, with us living separately in two different states, I really went into a relationship with blind eyes. When things seem too good to be true, always go with your first instinct.

I graduated from high school in 1977. After graduation William moved to Delaware. I took care of his mother for several years. When he realized what good care I was providing his mother, he took interest in me. I liked him but my main interest was to protect my daughter from his son. I figured if I married the father then she wouldn't marry her stepbrother.

Our marriage was strange, to say the least. I thought he must've been gay and married me as a front. That wasn't the case; he was using drugs instead. I entered into this marriage without getting guidance from the Lord. I married for the wrong reasons, so I had my faults also. Even though we grew up together and went to school and graduated the same year, I didn't meet this man until 21 years later. People change but I always look for the good in people. When he would travel from Wilmington to Berlin to see me, he would never have money to return to Wilmington and I would always financially aide his return trip. I should've questioned it but I didn't. For months he would come to visit me and it was always the same thing. I was helping his mother every day, I'm sure the family knew how he had changed and what problems he had. At the time, I didn't see any. Someone was actually interested in me, or so I thought.

We lived in Brookmont Farms, a low-income development. Because I was on disability and had one child living with me, my rent was $10 dollars a month for a two-bedroom townhouse. The townhouse was nice. William and I married at home, a month after moving to Delaware. Because my husband's uncle was a pastor, he officiated the ceremony. My husband had a stable job despite only buying beer every week when he got paid. I paid all the household bills and bought food for the house. Sometimes I used to think: *Oh my God, this is my third husband, and I'm in the same situation as the first and second husband.* I really can pick them, can't I?

My second husband was an alcoholic and a drug addict. He would steal money from me, my belongings, my bike, VCR and microwave. Anything he could pawn or sell for drugs. I was seven years older than him. His father, a deacon of a church, tried to sexually assault me. When I told my husband, he told me not to tell his mother because it would kill her. I thought my husband was sincere but I really didn't know him either. When I wouldn't give him money, he would tell his mom and say that I was telling lies about his dad. She had no idea what he was talking about; this was the first she'd ever heard of it. His mom said she didn't believe me because her husband was particular about his women. I told her he couldn't be too particular because he married her. Then it was time for me to pack a bag and leave, so off I went.

Now let's get back to husband number three. I was getting ready to leave for school one morning. I got dressed and headed out the front door and prepared to get into my car when I realized it had been stolen. At this point I knew I had to get away from this neighborhood. Brookmont was known for drugs and crime. I didn't know, but of course, my husband helped me find this place; I should've known. The police ended up finding my car in Philadelphia, stripped down with a damaged transmission. Out of a car and without transportation, God blessed me to move away from Brookmont and relocate to the suburbs of Newark. My husband decided to move with me because I was his meal ticket. He had a decent job at Delaware Park, a horse racing track and gambling casino. Even then he still only bought beer and paid for his weekly room rental at the YMCA. He paid for a room at the YMCA because he never knew when I was going to kick his lame ass out. Forgive me for my language.

Chapter 8

During my third marriage, I had Keon with me. Dear God, I didn't want my teenage son to watch this man use me. My son would likely tell you no man ever used his mom. I was both a mother and a father to my son. Keon was the child I was blessed to have. He's been my right hand and by my side through my long-term recovery. I love him with a mother's protective love. I sheltered him as a mother does a daughter; I was very protective, overprotective. I really wanted him to stay my baby until he grew up. He is a tall one though, clearly not a baby. Keon was my gift, the answer to my prayers. My gift Keon turned into a fine young man. Raising him was not easy, but with the Lord's help, I didn't do such a bad job. He has a heart of gold and is sort of quick-tempered when pushed. Other than that, he is kind and gentle. Keon has three lovely daughters and they love their dad. They are all daddy's little girls. He's the kind of father that puts his children first. His girls are babies now but just wait until their teenage years. I know they're going to be something.

Back to my life story. By the year 2000, I was still in my third marriage but it wasn't working out. I talked to God daily and asked him to reveal to me what I needed to know about this man. He really had no interest in me, just my disability income and a roof over his head. Well, one day I finally decided enough was enough.

Chapter 9

At the start of the new millennium, I was working at Pathmark and also taking a visiting nurses course. During this time, I had met the man that was about to change my whole life, Robert Sercelj. I met him when I first went to visiting nurses to sign up for the next course. God truly helps those who help themselves. One day after nursing class, a woman ran a red light and totaled my car. When I first met Bob, I asked him if we could we carpool together, who was a complete stranger at the time. After my car was totaled, I gave him a call and told him what had happened. For three months or more, he picked me up so that I could continue with my training.

During class we sat across from each other; I was fascinated by the way he would lift his false teeth up and roll them around in his mouth. He was intrigued by the determination I had to better myself. Bob and I carpooled all through the nursing course and on the last day he bought me a leather coat as a gift for completing the course.

After completing the last day of the nursing class, he dropped me off at home. I entered my apartment and I saw my husband going into the bathroom with a soda can. He didn't realize I was home. I opened the bathroom door and there he was, sitting on the toilet with a homemade pipe and a lighter getting ready to light up some crack cocaine. I said, "What are you doing?" William said, "What can I say? You done caught me." I prayed to God to reveal it to me, and after couple of years, God had answered my prayers. Thank you, Jesus, you answered my prayers. Now that I knew the truth, I threw him and his belongings out. If I'm going to do bad, I can do it all by myself. He was not helping me anyway, just using me; it hurt but I got rid of him and filed for divorce.

Konya Maria Crippen

My husband Francis holding Keon in his arms and me holding Konya.

A BLESSED SECOND CHANCE

Me, my sister Mona, and her daughter Kesha.

Konya Maria Crippen

In the kitchen with my daughter Konya.

A BLESSED SECOND CHANCE

My thirtieth birthday.

Konya Maria Crippen

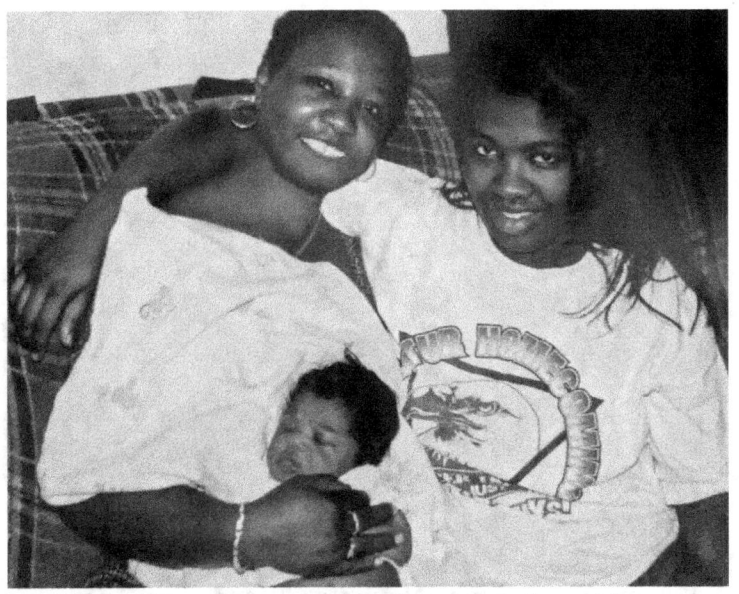

Me holding my granddaughter Teondra with my daughter Konya.

A BLESSED SECOND CHANCE

My son Keon with his daughters, Keona and Ayanna.

Konya Maria Crippen

Me and my son Keshawn. Not sure who's truck it was.

A BLESSED SECOND CHANCE

Bob and I after we got married.

Chapter 10

While I was waiting for my divorce proceedings to begin, Bob and I went out to dinner several times. For our first date, we went to St. Marks Church and enjoyed a chicken and dumpling dinner. We also spent time reading the Bible together. Everything we did, we made sure God was in the midst of it. Bob was born on November 30, 1942. I was born on November 25, 1959. Age did not matter nor race. Bob enjoyed taking pictures and I loved having my picture taken. I have hundreds of photos. I feel natural and beautiful when I'm being photographed. I'm not self-centered; I just enjoy modeling.

One Thanksgiving my son Keshawn came up to visit me. He caught the bus from Berlin. We picked him up at the bus station in Wilmington. Keshawn was around 16 or 17 years old at the time. We also invited an elderly man named Melvin to join us for Thanksgiving dinner. The man was sickly but he endured his sickness. I became very close to him and he was a dear friend. He more or less became like a father figure and mentor to me. He had two daughters and would always try to teach me how to become more ladylike. I was very country, still am.

We all had Thanksgiving dinner at my home: Bob, Keshawn, Melvin and me. After dinner Melvin left and we cleaned up from the meal. Keshawn had to be back in

Maryland by Monday so that he could get back home and go to school. He spent at least three days visiting during the holiday and he and Bob got to know each other better. When the time was getting close for Keshawn to return to Berlin, Bob took him to a used car dealership and paid cash to purchase a car for him so that he could drive himself back to Berlin instead of catching the bus. This was quite a surprise to me. I was making monthly payments on my car but Bob even paid my car off on the same day he bought my son's car. I couldn't help but be in awe of him.

As Bob and I spent more time getting to know each other, we spent time together going to church and reading the Bible. I even tried to give him myself intimately. Bob replied, "If I ever sleep with you, you'll never see me again." Wow, was this man for real? Yes, he was living a strictly Godly life and I know God found favor with him. He also helped me walk a straight path. I found favor with God also. On our first date, he bought me a bouquet of flowers from the church bazaar. It was purchased in 1991. To this day, I still have it.

Bob lived about two miles from me with his brother Frank. Bob and Frank were very close and looked very much alike. Bob and Keshawn spent time together whenever he came to visit. On one visit, Bob and Keshawn went to Christiana Mall and Bob bought me an engagement ring. I knew nothing about it. Then one-month Bob and Keshawn planned a dinner in Ocean City. Bob and I drove to Ocean City. As Keshawn and I were sitting down waiting for our order, Bob said, "Oh, I forgot the camera in the car." He went outside to get the ring. My son said to me, "Mom, Bob's going to propose to you; don't take the man's ring if you're not going to marry him." Again, I was in shock.

Finally, a man that loved me. Thank you, God. I couldn't believe it. We dated for two years and our wedding date was set for June 1, 2001. One day Bob came home with this purple evening dress. I thought to myself, *where am I ever going to wear this*? It was the second dress he had ever bought me. It was very formal and it hung in my closet for two years. I never realized that the dress would be my wedding dress. He told me he wanted me to feel like royalty. When we were dating, he would bring me roses, different colors every week. No man had ever done these things for me before. He gave me the finest of things. I loved it but I would have accepted dollar store deals and would have been just as pleased. I wanted him to see that I wasn't into material things. I would be thankful regardless. He could see that I was easy to please.

A BLESSED SECOND CHANCE

An attitude of love

Life presents us with challenges
That we must overcome
And sometimes all the detours
Can leave the sense numb
Life is filled with stumbling blocks
We pass along the way
But it can become a stepping stone
When love comes into play
Wherever there's an obstacle
That we must rise above
It helps to overcome it with
An attitude of love
For anger never solves a thing
And stress will bring us down
But love unlocks the doorway
Where hope and faith are found
So many things divide us
Throughout the human race
But love's the great uniter
The smile on mankind's face
Life presents us with challenges
That we must rise above
And blessed is he who can maintain
An attitude of love

Chapter 11

Bob, this amazing man, shared emotions with me and taught me how to love unconditionally. He accepted me for me and didn't want my body in return for all the goodness he showed me. This was different and a first for me. He treated me like the true lady that I am. Yet I still have my tom-boyish ways.

On June 1, 2001, I went to my girlfriend's house off of Maryland Avenue. She took me to have my hair done. Then we returned back to her house, where I got dressed for my wedding. Aurelia Pat Harvey was my maid of honor. Bob sent a limousine to pick us up that took us to the courthouse. Pat's husband was Bob's best man. Bob arrived at the courthouse and saw me with my hair done up for the first time; he told me it was beautiful.

We recited our vows:

(Robert): I Robert, take you Konya, for my lawfully wedded wife. To have and hold from this day forward, for better, for worse, for richer, for poorer, in sickness and in health, to love, to cherish, until death do us part.

(Konya): I Konya, take you Robert, for my lawfully wedded husband. To have and hold from this day forward, for better, for worse, for richer, for poorer, in sickness and in health, to love, to cherish, until death do us part.

A BLESSED SECOND CHANCE

(Robert): With this ring, I thee wed and pledge you my fidelity. Let it be a symbol of my love for you, now and forever.

(Konya): With this ring, I thee wed and pledge you my fidelity. Let it be a symbol for my love, for you, now and forever.

Chapter 12

As the years passed, our love for each other continued to grow stronger. We were there for each other always. We did everything together. I would even go with Bob and help out when he delivered meals on wheels.

In 2001, we went on our honeymoon to Bermuda. We took a cruise and left from New York. One year we went on vacation to Virginia Beach and I became sick. My husband took care of me. Once we returned back to Delaware, he took me straight to the hospital. On our third journey, my son Keshawn was stationed in Puerto Rico and invited us over for a week. Off we went to Puerto Rico. It was beautiful there. I felt like my son and I were getting closer but I was fooling myself.

My life with Bob is wonderful. Our marriage is solid. As a family, at times other than God, which is enough, all that we have is each other. Although stricken with liver cancer, my husband is my rock. When he gets out of bed at night, I'm his shadow. Within minutes I can tell his presence is gone. He can't move without me. This is my fourth husband, and God please forgive me, but this man is the first one that has truly been a husband to me. I'm happy and at peace. He has never mentally or physically abused me. Bob has never shown any signs of anger. Our marriage is good and I count every day as a blessing. My husband yields to me; he likes to satisfy me and keep me happy. I've never experienced a love that was so right. I don't have to worry about where he is because we are always together.

The years have gone by so quickly. As the saying goes, time flies when you're having fun. Being married to Bob is fun. We have so much love for each other it makes living together enjoyable. I never dreamed a man could love me the way my husband Bob does.

God had blessed us to see another year, 2009. Bob underwent chemotherapy twice this year. After his second treatment in 2009, the doctor said he could not have anymore. His veins had gotten too small. They put him on a trial chemotherapy pill called Nexavar. Bob started off taking two pills a day. The oncologist explained to him that he needed to take four pills a day 800mg each before the pills would have any effect. The pills are supposed to produce results similar to chemotherapy in the hospital. It prolongs life but your energy level is 0 to 1 on a scale of 1 to 10. What a life. You're just here, can't eat, don't want to do anything; you're just existing. Once my husband had enough, he told the doctor no more; he decided not to take the medicine anymore.

I started slipping them in with his other medications. Eventually I told him the truth; I just didn't want the cancer to spread. Then I had a talk with God and asked for his guidance and strength for the journey ahead.

Chapter 13

Bob gave me a 1998 Chrysler Cirrus. It is beautiful and I really cherish it. It has so much sentimental value to me. He drove this car when he gave me a ride back and forth to the visiting nurses classes. In 2002, Bob bought himself another car and he gave this one to me. I love it and I try to keep it as it was when I received it seven years ago. Ever since we met, I've always worked and enjoyed every day of it. Bob knew I wasn't like other women because material things didn't faze me. I liked nice things and would work hard to earn them even though I didn't have to.

God favored me when I met Bob. The one thing we shared the most was our love for the Lord. God was and is the start of everything. We read the Bible together, pray together, and everything we did God kept us through it all. Even though Bob was raised as a Catholic, he attended many different churches, mainly Baptist. He believed in God and he spent quality time with God's word.

Things change in our lives, along with the circumstances. Being of human nature you begin to doubt and question God. Bob was in turmoil; how could this happen to me? Not only was he in doubt but also the cancer had taken all of his joy and confidence. As I'm writing this, I can say there was a period in my life when

A BLESSED SECOND CHANCE

I was full of doubt and questions. But I got to know God and my Savior Jesus. Many prayers of the righteous were sent up for me. I gave my life to the Lord; for it was his from the start. God dwelling inside of me allowed his loving spirit to shine in my husband's darkest days. I told Bob over and over, "Bob I love you," sometimes 50 or more times a day. And I know he loved me.

Even today, God's love through his son Jesus is manifested because you never know what the future is going to bring. Bob had been going through treatments but he started throwing up blood on June 23, 2009. I rushed him to the hospital. When I brought Bob to the emergency room, I had my grandson Mekhi with me. I called Konya and told her she should come get her son. She agreed but stated she had to go home first. In the meantime, Frank, Bob's brother, came and I asked him to take Mekhi home until I got home that night. So he did. Mekhi had thrown a temper tantrum in the emergency room while Bob was being examined. He just didn't want to go with his mother. I tried to explain to my 10-year-old grandson that my husband comes first. With Bob under the same conditions, I kept Mekhi to help him cope and continued to spend daily time with my husband, as much time as I could. Although Bob was sick and incoherent, he knew I was by his side every day as long as I could be. Finally, he was discharged from the hospital and sent home with hospice care.

My faith is in God, not man. My testimony is that my husband had finished his work on earth. So, he was called home. I am at peace and I thank God every day for blessing me with a man that I could love and a husband that could love me for me. We were happy and loved each other so much, keeping Jesus as our first love. Our marriage was like a fairytale romance; however, life is a journey. Bob received his cancer diagnosis in 2004. For six years, he endured chemotherapy treatments. It kept him among the living but dead to life. You have either to go through it first hand or to have been a part of it to really understand what I'm speaking of. However, my love continued to grow stronger for Bob and I never wanted to leave his side.

Even though Bob was sent home from the hospital, a hospice nurse came to our home every day. I still enjoyed and spent every moment with my husband. At night, I would sleep on the couch so that I could be near him. Sometimes it was like our heartbeats were identical. We never argued or said an unkind word to each other. Bob always kept his thoughts to himself, even after he was diagnosed with cancer.

On February 10, 2010, Bob woke up around 2:00 AM urinating blood. Evidently, he had been bleeding from the nose and mouth as well. He was rushed to the hospital and diagnosed with internal bleeding. Doctors conducted multiple tests to see where the bleeding was coming from. Bob was banded on his veins and his esophagus. He spent three days in intensive care, a total of five days in the hospital. He was later released to go home under hospice care. He received morphine daily and was just existing. However, I continued to keep this scripture in mind: "Therefore I say unto you, What things soever ye desire, when ye pray, believe that ye receive them, and ye shall have them" (Mark 11:24 KJV).

A BLESSED SECOND CHANCE

Hospice would always tell me, "You need to tell your husband that you're going to be okay." Were they crazy? My faith and my denial would not let me do it. On March 12, 2010, after reading scriptures in the Bible, God strengthened me to tell my husband, "Bob, I love you, but God loves you more. If you're ready to go be with God, I want you to know I'll be alright."

Then he took a deep breath, his final breath, and closed his eyes. Gone for now but forever in my heart. I love you always.

I know Bob would not want me to stop living or to feel sorry for myself. My final wish was to tell him that I'd be alright. God has already showed me the strength that I possess through him. I can do all things through Christ that strengthens me. I found myself visiting his grave site every day, sometimes twice a day. I continued praying and talking to God. Through time he answered me in many ways. Mainly saying "Stay focused on me; I will never leave nor forsake you." I then started going back to church. During the time that I felt helpless, God showed me how to invest in myself and others. I could hear Him say, "Help yourself, while helping someone else." "In all thy ways acknowledge him, and he shall direct thy paths" (Proverbs 3:6 KJV).

I tried to find work but was not successful, so I applied for disability. God blessed me and I was approved. Thank God! I at least had rent money. Because I still believed I needed to do something with my life, I contacted vocational rehabilitation to start a new chapter in my life.

Chapter 14

Don't grieve for me, for now I'm free
I'm following the path God laid for me
I took his hand when I heard his call
I turned my back and left it all
I couldn't stay another day
To laugh, to love, to work, to play
Task left undone must stay that way
I've found that peace at the end of the day
If parting has left a void
Please fill it with remembered joy
A kind friendship, a shared laugh, a kiss
And yes, these things too will I miss
Be not burdened with times of sorrow
I wish you sunshine of tomorrow
My life's been full, I savored much
Good people, good times, a loved one's touch
Perhaps my time seemed all too brief
Don't lengthen it now with undue grief
Lift up your heart and share with me
God wanted me now, he set me free

Chapter 15

Today is March 28, 2018. Thank you, father, for another day that you have blessed me to see. Every day since you brought me out of a coma and healed my body from a stroke, I have counted the days as blessings. Whatever sufferings I have to endure, Lord, here I am. I never stop praying for the children you've blessed me with. Konya, Keon and Keshawn. Thank you, father. Even after coming out of the coma to later having a stroke, my children remained my purpose for living. In my heart, that's the way it was always going to be until a pastor told me otherwise. He said, "No my child; God has to be number one, then your children." I prayed and I'm still praying. Keshawn was only a few months old and is now 36 years old. Keon who was 3 is now 39 years old, and Konya who was 6 is now 42 years old. All of them have children, which has blessed me with ten grandchildren. God, I thank you. Even through all my sins, you still love me and still bless me. Lord, all my trials and tribulations have brought me closer to your will and your way. My newest grandchild Shawnie was born earlier this year. I am also blessed to have two God-gifted, intelligent, smart and beautiful daughter in-laws, Desiree and Jess. I thank my heavenly father for every second of life. Life is a gift, freely given through the death of Jesus Christ. Through prayers and my faith God is mending the relationship between my children and me. We're not as close as I'd like but I'm thankful. I can truthfully say God does answer prayers. He answers prayers on His time, not ours. I say again wait on the Lord and be of good courage. God has blessed me to see all of my children reach their adulthood. Every day all of them are still in my prayers. From my personal experiences, I know God does answer prayers.

In 2007, I received a job at Delaware Park, a horse racing casino in Wilmington Delaware. While working there I met the next man to become a part of my life, Bill Channell. I left Delaware Park in 2009 so that I could be with my husband Bob during his fight against cancer. Bob died in 2010. *Oh my God*, I thought, *here I am again, alone, depressed, living in the same apartment that my deceased husband and I shared for nine years*. Months after his death, I started gambling. Not to get rich, just to get out and be among people. I soon found myself $20,000 in debt, gambling and using cash from my credit cards.

One day I went over to the casino. Upon leaving Bill, a security guard asked me for my phone number. The date was March 24, 2015, a Tuesday morning. Years before Bill and I both worked as security guards at Delaware Park. I used to have a keychain that read, *Here is my number, 1-800-GET LOST*. Whenever any male approached me asking for my phone number, I would always flash my keychain. But not this time. Besides, he had beautiful blue eyes and he was bowlegged. I love that in a man. Anyway, I gave Bill my number. We had been co-workers for three years, so we already knew each other from work. It had been five years since my husband had died and I had closed myself off from men.

After giving Bill my number, he didn't call right away. Finally, after sitting by my phone day after day, the phone rang and his name appeared on my caller ID. We talked on the phone, learning little things about each other. I was still very cautious but at the same time very happy. We would talk on the phone every day. If you hadn't realized it already, I am a go-getter. During the summer of 2015, I would drive to New Jersey every Sunday after church service to get crabs. On my way home, I would always stop at the Family Dollar store in Pennsville, New Jersey. Bill told me that he lived a couple of blocks behind that shopping center. One day I was on my way to Marty's for crabs when I took a chance and called him. He was at home and gave me directions to his house. When I arrived, he was surprised, but this was only the beginning. He took me to Fort Mott Park. We walked around the park holding hands and getting to know each other better.

Because I am a very independent woman, it takes a very strong-minded man to deal with me. That is one of the qualities I love in Bill. He has a heart of gold. He even cared for his mother, who passed away from lung cancer. That is another thing we have in common. We were caregivers to our loved ones until death. He cooks. He's funny, kind, handsome and spoiled. He also likes to have things his way. I fall in love with him, more and more each time I'm with him. There's never a dull moment. I love you and accept you just as you are, Bill, with whatever baggage that comes along with you. NO ONE

IS PERFECT: Love me for me, if you can, if you can't, God has me and it's all good.

In September of 2015, I moved in with Bill. We took a house he used only for sleeping, or should I say a bachelor pad, and cleaned it up and made it into a home. We've had some rough, rocky times, but the good has always outweighed the bad. He has been so good to me; I can be a real handful at times. As I said in the beginning, it takes a very strong man to deal with me. Bill has loved me through it all. I know his love for me is genuine. Thank you, God; you've blessed me yet again. He gave me my engagement and wedding ring set on Christmas Day.

We are still learning one another. It's been almost a year since we've been dating and I've been living with him for five months. However, I'm a Christian saved by grace. We live together without being intimate. This is the way it will remain until we are legally married. He doesn't force the issue but instead accepts how I feel. Now that's true love. Can you tell me what man is going to put his home up as collateral so that I can get a $20,000 loan to get out of debt and is not receiving sex in exchange? Now I know this is yet another blessing from God.

We are both bullheaded, however, and we both want our way about things. But every couple has their ups and downs. I pray a lot and ask my heavenly father for his guidance. I'm trying to live a Godly life. There is no perfection in the world, save Jesus Christ only. God has blessed me to still be amongst the living. As I write about this part of my life, I'm now 58 years old. In November

A BLESSED SECOND CHANCE

2018, I will be 59. To God I give all the praise. I can do all things through Christ that strengthens me. In therapy and rehabilitation, and mainly my faith in God, I took the word *can't* out of my vocabulary. I'm a very positive person. Things people say I can't do God gives me the strength to do. I've learned to live by the golden rule treat others the way you want to be treated. I let go and let God work through me. I love everybody. JESUS SHINES THROUGH ME.

I now live in Pennsville, a nice calm, violence free town. Everyone in this town is either a senior citizen or a child. Everyone keeps to themselves. As for me, you can be a stranger and I'll still go an extra mile to be of assistance. Just a smile or a warm good morning can brighten someone's world. I've learned how to love even while hurting. With God all things are possible. I know my life is witness to his goodness and power. Sometimes in our lives we are tested. But I ask the Lord to give me the strength to endure. God knows our every thought, pain, everything; there's nothing he does not already know. I will not let Satan steal my joy. The past cannot be changed but the future can and will be better.

When Bill and I started to get to know each other, I never thought I'd meet someone going through problems in life much similar to mine. He cared for his mother until lung cancer stole her life. I cared for my husband until liver cancer took his life. Thank you, God, again; you kept me. You promised to never leave or forsake me and you haven't. I love you Lord. Continue to mold me; shape me in your image.

As for Bill, he has a heart of gold and tries to display a tough exterior, but underneath it all, he's my spoiled brat. I've never had a man that could cook from scratch, and after eating his cooking, it's better than anything I've ever had. Lasagna, vegetable chicken soup, cheesesteak subs, meatloaf, you name it. He says his mother taught him; in case he ever was alone, he would be able to take care of himself. And he can even though I keep telling him we can do nothing without God.

I've learned how to be content and forgiving and how to trust God and keep the faith. I have 10 grandchildren. This is another blessing that God has gifted me with. The oldest is 24 years old and the youngest is 10 months old. Shawnie was named after his father Keshawn. Easter 2018 my son Keshawn stopped in to see me on his way to another military base in north New Jersey. He has been in the Navy since 2002. His rank is Senior Chief. My God, here is another blessing. He is now 36 years old, married and a father of three handsome sons. This time spent with him this Easter was an answer to my prayers, something I'd been praying for. Not in my time, but thy will be done. Every day is a blessing and a gift, whatever the day holds. I always remember this is a day the Lord made; I shall rejoice and be glad in it.

Not even pain in my body can take the joy that God has given me away. I'm so proud of how my sons have God in their lives. I have two sons and they are the best dads any child could hope for. They give their children the love, support and time their children need. My daughter Konya is also a God fearing, mother who has raised three children on her own. I'm proud of all my children. I never stop praying and God, my father, never stops answering prayers. Through the years, I've tried to establish a relationship with my first born. Each time I open my heart, its broken worse than before.

However, my father God always puts my brokenness back together, making me stronger than before. I love you Konya and always will. You were my gift from God; you were a blessing given to me on September 11, 1976, after nine months of a high-risk pregnancy. Like Charlie Wilson's song: Ask me how I am. I'm blessed. Pain, heartache, disappointment, I'm blessed. Nothing can take my joy away. Konya, Keon and Keshawn, all of you were gifts from God. If I've done anything that I shouldn't have, I ask for your forgiveness. All of you have made me so proud; I thank God he chose me to be the female vessel to give life to you.

Last year my fiancé had a knee replacement. I watched him go through pain and therapy as he recovered. Thank you, God, for allowing me to be of Godly assistance and physical assistance. Each time either one of us sees a doctor, we're always together supporting one another in love. We do everything together, even argue or disagree, but love always wins. Faith, hope and love, but the greatest of these is love. Love always overcomes any obstacle in life you may face. Every day of my life, I'm physically in pain but God promised he would put no more on me than I could bare. Every day I thank God for everything. I take every ache with a joyful smile. Our life is a mystery to us, but not to God. My life as of now, other than pain in my body, is fine.

After five years following my husband's death, Bill and I became a couple. We are very much alike, yet different. He has a heart that's so caring and kind. He tries to be outspoken but God gave me a voice and I too am outspoken at times. It's all good because the both of us were unable to raise our children from birth; both of us can understand the heartache and feelings of rejection that came from having our family ripped from us, on no part of our own. Mine is getting better, while a part of Bill's is still tearing his world apart inside.

I thank God for putting me as a mate in his life. He is a caring, loving man. We adopted a kitten in June. I named him after my grandson Joshua. He has brought so much joy to our lives. He acts just like a human child. He is also spoiled, so for now we are raising Joshua Kojak Channell. He weighed two pounds when we first brought him home; now he weighs 14 pounds and is 25 inches long. His height reminds me of my son Keon. This year I have two granddaughters graduating from high school. Keona and Gigi, my daughter's baby girl. I was able to be a part of Keona's life as she grew up through the years. As for Gigi, I was a part of her life when she was a baby. The only thing I can say is when you take a grandparent from a child you are hurting the child more than you know. Even this I pray about; vengeance is mine saith the Lord. Trying to repay evil, never works. I've learned that LOVE CONQUERS ALL.

Through all of my obstacles, afflictions and rejections, I continue to look up, from which cometh my help. All of my help comes from God my father and Jesus my Savior. I'm still having my share of trials and tribulations; I won't let it break me but I'll use it as a strengthener. Pain is not easy, neither is heartache. At times I don't understand but somehow, I endure. With God all things are possible. I used to question God but no more. Even today my heart was ripped in pieces. Lord, I still thank you through it all. No weapon formed against me shall prosper. I learned to pray, give it to God and let go. Life is a mystery and I've learned to take it one day at a time. In April, I was diagnosed with torn ligaments in my right knee; I won't use this as an excuse but rather count it as a blessing. God is telling me to slow down and take it easy. The pain is so severe but I deal with it and try not to let it stop me from my daily routine of life. Although it is very painful, I can barely walk. I can do all things through Christ that strengthens me. I'm looking to God from which all my help comes.

From this day June 8, 2018, I will not focus on my past for it is behind me. I will speak of now, through my trials, tribulations, heartache, and physical afflictions; I will allow it all to strengthen me. I will remain positive, giving God the praise through it all. On June 12, 2018, I had a scope operation on my right knee. Thank God, I'm now walking better and pain-free in my knee. I have several ruptured discs in my back in addition to arthritis throughout my body. I've had steroid injections in my back, which allows me to be pain-free.

On June 19, 2018, Bill and I adopted two more kittens: TC and Ahmad. Bill has spoiled them; they sleep on his chest and legs. Ahmad weighs maybe a quarter of a pound and TC weighs about half of a pound. Meanwhile, Joshua weighs 14 pounds and is maintaining his castle, constantly keeping Joshua from attacking the other kittens. They move fast as lightning, so I'm losing weight chasing and keeping up with them. It's a full-time job.

Today is the second day of summer. I'm almost painless, but I'm still in debt and I must work until I'm out of this situation that I got myself into. Only God and I can comprehend it. Next time I'll know better. Life is still good. I have peace of mind and love. The devil will not destroy what God has given me. God has truly blessed me; all of my children are grown and are caring, loving parents. If I could live my life over, I'd show them I, too, was a caring loving single-parent. Working day and night trying to provide for them. My daughter's father denied being her father and my husband dealt drugs. He had a dangerous life and he tried to provide for his sons by making fast money. But I still loved him. I guess being young I did not look at life the way I do now. If only I had known God the way I do now. My mother died when I was only 15 years old. A baby having a baby, Mom did her best raising five children as a single- parent. All four of my sisters and I are very much like Mom: hard- working, doing our best to survive, not depending on any human being, faithfully trusting God for all things. Mom did not depend on a man; I can truthfully say none of us do. We're tough, stubborn, hardheaded and very independent. *What have I gotten myself into*? I keep asking myself this question but can't seem to find the answer. All of us have a purpose in life, so this must be mine. Lord, I just pray for your guidance, for you know all things.

A BLESSED SECOND CHANCE

On July 12, 2018, I logged onto the computer to see pictures from my niece's birthday. After wishing Dachanda a happy blessed birthday, I later found out that she is planning her son's funeral, her first born. I can feel her hurt and loss. My God, I pray that you give her strength and courage through this difficult and trying time. Surround her with your heavenly angels and let her know although she loved her son you loved him more. What this world has to offer is nothing compared to the heavenly paradise you have awaiting him. He is with you. Sweetie, the heartache you feel, I wish I could spare you. Just know our heavenly father knows best.

We don't understand but our heavenly father does. Our prayers aren't always answered in the way we ask them but the outcome is always for the best. God will not put more on you than you can bare. Each day I thank God for all my blessings. God is so good. Getting close to being blessed to reach the age of 59. Thank you, Lord and Savior of my life. It's all been and is a blessing.

Chapter 16

Each morning as the Lord awakes me, I thank Him for just another day of life. Even with all the pain in my body and other disappointments in life that come daily. I hold my head up and smile and continue to move on awaiting the next challenge, or should I say tribulation of my journey through life. I love life and want to live up to whatever God expects of me. It's not easy but he never said life would be. When I was young, I did not know the things that I know now. I'm wiser and use my knowledge mainly to inspire or help others. This book is dedicated to my family, my children, Keshawn, Keon and daughter Konya. Also, my sisters, nieces, nephews and grandchildren. I'm blessed with so many.

I love you all and pray that I can inspire you to get all that life has to offer, along with God's promises. Never give up on the goals you wish to accomplish. You can reach for the highest dream and allow it to come true. No pain no gain; pain only causes me to strive harder to accomplish my goal. People used to say to me, "You're disabled." I would reply, "No, I'm physically challenged." My body may not function like a normal person but my mind and brain do. God has me and my faith is strong. I can do all things through Christ that strengthens me. Obstacles in life come every day but I keep pushing forward. Life is a journey and life is beautiful. I would not change a thing. This story is a true testament of my life and how God has saved me from death's door, how a seed planted in my life continues to blossom.

I know God is not through with me yet. Faith as small as a mustard seed can move mountains. Here are some Bible verses that continue to keep me steadfast along my journey: "The fear of the Lord is the beginning of knowledge, but fools despise wisdom and instruction" (Proverbs 1:7 KJV). "I have taught thee in the way of wisdom; I have led thee in right paths" (Proverbs 4:11 KJV). When thou goest, thy steps shall not be straightened; and when thou runnest, thou shalt not stumble" (Proverbs 4:12 KJV). My life? "Not that I speak in respect of want; for I have learned, in whatsoever state I am, therewith to be content" (Philippians 4:11 KJV). "Now unto God and our Father be glory for ever and ever. Amen" (Philippians 4:20 KJV). God's got me and He's been there through it all. Ask me how I am. I'm blessed. To God be all glory and honor. And Jesus Savior of the world.

Psalm 91 (KJV)

He that dwelleth in the secret place of the most High shall abide under the shadow of the Almighty.
I will say of the Lord, He is my refuge and my fortress: my God; in him will I trust.
Surely he shall deliver thee from the snare of the fowler, and from the noisome pestilence.
He shall cover thee with his feathers, and under his wings shalt thou trust: his truth shall be thy shield and buckler.
Thou shalt not be afraid for the terror by night; nor for the arrow that flieth by day;
Nor for the pestilence that walketh in darkness; nor for the destruction that wasteth at noonday.
A thousand shall fall at thy side, and ten thousand at thy right hand; but it shall not come nigh thee.
Only with thine eyes shalt thou behold and see the reward of the wicked.
Because thou hast made the Lord, which is my refuge, even the most High, thy habitation;
There shall no evil befall thee, neither shall any plague come nigh thy dwelling.
For he shall give his angels charge over thee, to keep thee in all thy ways.
They shall bear thee up in their hands, lest thou dash thy foot against a stone.

A BLESSED SECOND CHANCE

Thou shalt tread upon the lion and adder: the young lion and the dragon shalt thou trample under feet.

Because he hath set his love upon me, therefore will I deliver him: I will set him on high, because he hath known my name.

He shall call upon me, and I will answer him: I will be with him in trouble; I will deliver him, and honour him.

With long life will I satisfy him, and shew him my salvation.

Psalm 119: 65-72 (KJV)

Thou hast dealt well with thy servant, O Lord, according unto thy word.
Teach me good judgment and knowledge: for I have believed thy commandments.
Before I was afflicted I went astray: but now have I kept thy word. Thou art good, and doest good; teach me thy statutes.
The proud have forged a lie against me: but I will keep thy precepts with my whole heart.
Their heart is as fat as grease; but I delight in thy law.
It is good for me that I have been afflicted; that I might learn thy statutes.
The law of thy mouth is better unto me than thousands of gold and silver.

www.ingramcontent.com/pod-product-compliance
Lightning Source LLC
Chambersburg PA
CBHW071414290426
44108CB00014B/1814